Phoenix Flame

Overcoming Devastation by Rising Again

By: *Forest of Truth*

THE ASHES

What once was whole is now undone.

In smoke and silence, greed has won.

This is the place of endings... and ache.

The weight is real. The fire takes.

The Collapse

One day it cracked with no warning.
What held me, gave beneath my feet.
No storm, no sign, just a sudden fall,
As if the world forgot to hold me at all.

My name, my plans, the shape of how to cope.
All crumbled quiet, nothing left but smoke.
The timeline blinked, memory went still.
My bones felt fear before my will.

I didn't scream. I didn't run.
Just watched the scaffolds come undone.
The life I wore peeled off like skin.
No way to fix what broke within.

The Fog

I wandered through rooms without corners,
Where silence posed as care.
Each voice wore a clinical smile,
Polished, professional, bare.

My pulse thudded questions unanswered.
The walls leaned in, unsure.
The world spun in slow repetitions,
Through doors I'd walked before.

They said I looked fine in the mirror,
But even the glass lied.
I carried a truth they couldn't hold,
It vanished each time I tried.

Opportunity Costs

They handed us stories full of holes,
And maps with missing lines.
Their myths were stitched from silence,
Their egos disguised as spine.

We drank from wells with bitter roots,
Ate fruit that gleamed with lies.
The seeds they sowed grew shiny skins,
But whispered poisoned skies.

Still in the soil, a reckoning hum,
A tremble in the grain.
Some wounds are wrapped in blossoms,
But bloom as heat and pain.

Stillness

Not every end makes noise.
Some vanish, steam rising from tin.
What breaks us doesn't always scream.
Sometimes, simply stopping from within.

The body ceases motion.
The world keeps spinning past.
Their hands so cold and still.
Will truth be told at last?

I learned the sound of nothing.
How breath can be dense like a rock.
No answers to surface for years.
Only stillness, can hold up to the clock.

The Weight

You do not forget the weight.
Even when you stand again.
Some loads were never yours to carry.
Yet they drag you till you bend.

This might bare, if you get stronger.
But how strong must one become?
Body breaks and heart is lonely.
Holding grief that bounds your lungs.

You smile, and no one questions.
They can't see what you withstand,
But pain made you resilient.
Rise again, without a hand.

The Spark

From deepest dark, a flicker dares.
A breath, a pull, a thread of prayers.
The silence stirs. The ember wakes.
In quiet calm, the kindle waits.

First Light

I did not wait for the sun.
I moved when shadows said to "stay."
A flicker far off, maybe hope, maybe not,
Reason enough to seek the way.

I followed cracks in broken walls,
Let moonlight show the haze.
Some steps were crawling. Some were still.
Always a way out from the maze.

You do not need to feel the fire,
To know warmth can return.
The smallest light can guide you home,
If you dare to let it burn.

A Question Forms

A flicker hums behind the noise,
A whisper rising from your chest.
You thought the candle was your guide,
New light now gives it rest.

It's not a shout, nor clear command,
Just... knowing, deep within.
A statement forms without a sound:
The answer's always been.

You pause. You breathe. You turn your face.
A voice once buried now feels near.
The dark remains, less alone, you echo.
"Where you always here?"

The Stranger Within

A glance, a breath, you almost missed.
Underneath your face and fears.
Not shaped by shame, nor bent by wants,
Simply watching, gaze sincere.

You blink. You shift. You hold the stare.
Presence warm, not pushing in.
No stranger now, this soul you see,
Is known beneath the skin.

No mirror gave this view before.
No name is needed here.
Just you, beneath the world's disguise,
Still whole. Still brave. Still near.

Refusal to Give Up

I didn't know which way to go.
The sky was black, the ground unsure.
My mind went numb, my hope withdrew,
Yet something moved me to endure.

No logic lit that choking dark,
Still lost, the path unclear.
But yet I paused... and breathed again,
With breath that tastes like fear.

It wasn't only will, or strength,
Something deep and out of sight.
The silent voice that whispered loud:
You will survive the night.

Unspoken Yes

I didn't shout, I didn't cry.
No vow declared beneath the sky.
But deep inside, a knowing stirred,
No lightning flash, no final word.

I simply breathed and didn't stop.
The fear was loud, the hope was not.
Yet in the quiet, something changed,
Not forced by will, not praise, not strain.

A yes was given, soft and true.
To follow what I barely knew.
Not to be easy, but to agree.
To rise, and walk, and choose to be.

THE FLAME

Light meets resistance, truth burns through.
In heat, the old shape shatters too.
This fire is pain—and holy birth.
Once lost, the truth becomes your worth.

Kindling

I did not feel the fire yet.
Just warmth beneath the ache.
A soft, persistent stirring,
Where nothing used to wake.

No blaze, no burst of fury,
Just hands that flexed again.
The will to move was distant,
But not as far as then.

I stacked my breath like branches.
I let the silence spark.
You don't need flame to start the burn.
Just embers in the dark.

Friction

I knew too much to turn around.
But still wore habits like old skin.
My voice was changing, yet I spoke.
The way I always had within.

I tried to shrink inside the fire,
Pretend the truth was just a phase.
But ashes itched beneath my clothes,
And light kept leaking through the haze.

I wasn't ready. Still, I burned.
The self I knew began to slip.
Resistance pulled like rope across my ribs.
But every knot began to rip.

Awakening Body

I used to live outside my skin.
A ghost in bones I didn't trust.
Numbness was a safer ground,
Than feeling what the falsehoods crushed.

But something stirred beneath the ribs.
A pulse I hadn't known was mine.
My breath grew heavy, wide, and wild,
Like wind reclaiming fallen pines.

The ache returned, but heat was warming.
My hands began to grip the real.
It hurt to feel, but more to stay,
A stranger to what I knew could heal.

Firewalk

The fire didn't ask if I was ready.
It only opened up a path.
Each step was pain, yet I moved forward.
Burned higher when trying to go too fast.

The heat exposed what I had hidden.
Old wounds flared like open flame.
I felt the truth against my skin.
It called me forward just the same.

No strength carried me above this fire.
It was strength that made me stay.
Through trust in what the burn might clear,
And something holy in the blaze.

Molting

It didn't fall all at once.
My old self peeled like paper.
Each flake a fear, a role, a mask.
Torn soft, not sharp like razors.

I wore it long beyond its life.
It stretched, then split, then stung.
My body knew before I did,
The shape of who I'd become.

No glory in the shedding.
No spotlight, no parade.
Just me, alone and trembling,
And finally less afraid.

The Inferno

Nowhere left to run or hide.
The shadows speak, seen self divide.
We cannot wait, simply aspire.
The only way is through the fire.

The Mirror Breaks

I thought I'd faced the worst of me,
The glass had only shown my face.
Beneath the grin, behind those eyes,
Waited something I'd misplaced.

It wasn't rage that scared me most,
But all the ache I'd locked away.
Grief with teeth. Fear without name.
Bearing learned to smile and stay.

I did not shatter with the mirror.
I stood and watched it fall apart.
And in the cracks, I met myself.
Still breath and a beating heart.

Burning Clean

I carried grief like coals in cloth.
Too hot to hold, too close to drop.
Shame hissed in corners of my mind,
Rage waited for when breath would stop.

The fire didn't judge the thoughts.
It only asked I let it burn.
And so I let it one by one,
The names, the lies, to the return.

I thought release would feel like calm,
But it began with something mean.
Until the smoke began to clear.
And what remained was burning clean.

Howl

I had no words for what I felt.
Pressure seeping into bone.
So much endured in silence,
I forgot I wasn't stone.

Then fear turned ice, grief turned storm,
And something primal broke the air.
Feelings I thought weren't meant for words.
Are the proof I was still there.

No one came to hush the noise.
None I'd allow to make it small.
I howled until the dagger shifted,
The aching softened after all.

Ashes of Control

I tried to hold the shape that was.
But fire doesn't keep a mold.
The tighter grip to who I'd been,
The quicker everything turned cold.

Control had once been how I coped.
Perfection was my shield.
But in the flame, it fell away,
What's authentic was revealed.

I knelt despite the burn at last.
Not broken, not undone.
I whispered, "Help me find the way."
That's the day healing begun.

Nothing to Fear

I felt the fire underneath my skin.
The horizon still burned, I stood still.
I met the dark without my armor,
And found it softened to my will.

The fear I carried wasn't needed.
Just smoke clinging to what I'd known.
Beneath the ash, I felt my footing,
And realized that I was not alone.

It wasn't that the pain had gone.
But I no longer tried to flee.
I knew what lived inside the flame,
And it no longer frightened me.

THE REBIRTH

From soot and soil, the roots push wide.
New breath, new blood, a rising tide.
A walk with steps taken in pride.
The body remembers, I'm alive.

Sapling

I do not leap. I do not fight.
I press one toe into the ground.
The world is soft but holds me now,
Enough to rise with new truth found.

My roots are new, but still they reach.
I feel the sun with rougher skin.
No need to bloom before I breathe,
No need to prove that I can win.

No longer who was in the fire.
New seeds begin to fall.
They crack the earth from deep inside,
And dare, to grow at all.

Remembering Health

Health felt like something to be earned.
A prize for perfect ways.
But healing came through memory,
Not judgment, force, or praise.

My body didn't need perfection,
Just space to be and feel.
A warmth returned where pain once lived.
Not sudden, but finally real.

I listened not to fear this time.
Something older, soft and wise.
The map was written in my bones,
Health never lost, just disguised.

Soil and Sun

I used to fight the world to grow.
Thought I alone could mend the break.
But then I touched the roots beneath.
Felt the Earth's heartbeat quake.

The trees, the ground, the quiet wind,
Whispering, *you're not alone.*
The sun did not demand my strength.
It warmed me as I softened home.

I learned that rest can feed the spark,
Soil holds memory and waits.
And healing grows not just within,
But all around, in time and space.

Threaded Together

I thought healing meant becoming whole,
Alone, untouched, and strong.
But growth arrived like woven thread.
A pattern missing all along.

I felt your truth before I saw you.
A glance, a nod, and silent grace.
Our scars did not compete for prizes.
They meld as rivers in one space.

The self I built, both mine and ours,
Sinking deeper than the dew.
We're not meant to rise apart.
The heart repairs where threads run through.

Born Again

No thunder marked the moment.
No words descended from the sky.
But something deep inside grew still,
And I remembered to reply.

Not to be better, totally healed.
Just true, discerned, and kind.
The fire taught me why to learn.
The soil gave me back my mind.

I didn't rise for anyone.
Didn't need to prove or plan.
I simply breathed and felt myself.
Born again, able to stand.

THE GLOW

Warmth returns. The fire tamed.
Light shines on skin, not just the flame.
Life no longer hurts to hold.
The weak renewed, becomes the bold.

Radiance

It came without announcement.
A softness in the light.
Not pride, but a quiet glow.
That made the world feel right.

My face looked older in the mirror,
But it had made it through the storm.
No longer chasing perfect.
Just grateful for what's warm.

I didn't rise in lace of gold.
I simply came to be.
And in that still, forgiving light,
I saw the beauty grow in me.

Walking Softly

I no longer chase the morning.
I walk it barefoot, slow.
My pace is not from anguish,
But from everything I know.

I've burned. I've begged. I've stumbled.
I've risen with no crown.
I do not need to take up space.
I'm space I stand in now.

No performance and no armor.
Just steady breath and ground.
There is a kind of strength in peace.
Power lives in softness found.

The Gift of Slowness

I used to fight the morning.
As if peace could be won.
But wellness came with quiet feet,
And lingered in the sun.

I learned to move like branches.
To wait without alarm.
The world did not forget me,
Just because I've faced the harm.

Slowness is a ceremony.
Each breath a kind return.
There is balance in doing less,
And trusting what I've learned.

Held and Holding

There were days I couldn't lift myself,
And hands arrived without a word.
They didn't push, or force a fix.
They stayed, and helped, and heard.

Now I know what care looks like.
A glance, a smile, a shared exhale.
We heal in turns, not order.
We lift each other through the veil.

I walk with ones still aching.
I rest when others lead the way.
We're not whole, until together,
Love is where we're meant to stay.

Alive Still

I do not rush to name it.
This calm feeling from within.
It's not a high, or shining peak,
But something settled in.

I rest with no apology.
I rise without regret.
There's beauty now in quiet days.
Let go, to not forget.

I do not sparkle every step,
Or need to chase a thrill.
I'm here, experiencing life.
I'm alive, and being still.

THE SOAR

No longer bound, no longer small.
Wings stretch wide. I answer the call.
The sky is mine. The ground forgives.
Within me: truth, joy, love, all lives.

Lift Off

I didn't leap to prove I could.
Lifting when it felt like time.
The weight had lessened, bit by bit,
Until the sky was mine.

No one declared me worthy.
No cell was marked release.
I simply felt the space expand,
And stepped into my peace.

Not high above, but moving now,
The wind beneath me true.
It wasn't that I learned to fly.
Just stopped gripping what I knew.

Clear Eyes

I used to see through goggles.
Fogged by fear and old belief.
The world looked sharp, then shapeless,
Colored most by fear and grief.

But something in me shifted.
A lens I didn't know had cracked.
I blinked and saw the light tilt,
As color all rushed back.

The sky was never only gray.
I'd just forgotten how it bends.
With clear eyes, I saw the truth.
Your view can shift as the heart mends.

Trailblazer

I no longer trek to prove I can.
I lead because I've walked the fire.
My voice is shaped by power now,
Strength no longer built from ire.

I don't demand that others follow.
I do not fear to go alone.
The path ahead is far but real.
Marked by roots that became known.

I carry the light, not outright,
But as something we have earned.
And those who walk behind me,
Will find the way the trail has turned.

Joy Unshaken

I've tasted peace that doesn't flee.
Harnessed the fire and the pain.
A quiet joy now lives in me,
Not loud like laughter, deep like rain.

It doesn't live in perfect days,
Or promise not to break.
It roots itself in wiser ways,
In all I've learned, in what I take.

I'm smiling as the storm rolls on.
Not as denial, but through grace.
This joy is steady in my soul.
The fire stays, and lights this place.

Flightpath

The winds no longer push me down,
Rising with wings I chose and skill.
Not running from what I left behind,
But moving with my own true will.

The sky ahead is vast and wide,
No map or guarantee in hand.
Trust and intentions deep inside,
With peace in what I understand.

No longer lost, misunderstood.
Path of values, clear and true.
The fire I tend will gently last,
And light the way I'm flying to.

Thank you

I hope this book has lit a spark,
a warmth for your journey ahead.

With gratitude

Forest of Truth

Authors Note:

This book was written for anyone who
has experienced significant difficulty,
with special care for those navigating
chronic health challenges.

May these pages offer
acknowledgment,
a sense of **possibility**,
and **peacefulness**
to all who feel drawn
to its message.

You are not alone.
We can continue sharing our stories,
learning from each other, and healing.

Forest of Truth

If this message resonated with you,

You can help others find this book by leaving a review:

Phoenix inspired 100% organic cotton t-shirts are available at:

www.ingramcontent.com/pod-product-compliance
Lightning Source LLC
LaVergne TN
LVHW010027070426

835513LV00001B/1